POETRY Wonderland

East Yorkshire

Edited By Brixie Payne

First published in Great Britain in 2019 by:

Young Writers®
Est. 1991

Young Writers
Remus House
Coltsfoot Drive
Peterborough
PE2 9BF
Telephone: 01733 890066
Website: www.youngwriters.co.uk

All Rights Reserved
Book Design by Ashley Janson
© Copyright Contributors 2018
SB ISBN 978-1-78988-039-7
Printed and bound in the UK by BookPrintingUK
Website: www.bookprintinguk.com
YB0386N

FOREWORD

Here at Young Writers, we love to let imaginations run wild and creativity go crazy. Our aim is to encourage young people to get their creative juices flowing and put pen to paper. Each competition is tailored to the relevant age group, hopefully giving each pupil the inspiration and incentive to create their own piece of creative writing, whether it's a poem or a short story. By allowing them to see their own work in print, we know their confidence and love for the written word will grow.

For our latest competition Poetry Wonderland, we invited primary school pupils to create wild and wonderful poems on any topic they liked – the only limits were the limits of their imagination! Using poetry as their magic wand, these young poets have conjured up worlds, creatures and situations that will amaze and astound or scare and startle! Using a variety of poetic forms of their own choosing, they have allowed us to get a glimpse into their vivid imaginations. We hope you enjoy wandering through the wonders of this book as much as we have.

CONTENTS

Broadacre Primary School, Hull

Christine Hua Vong (10)	1
Ruby Jay Scarah (10)	3

Cottingham Croxby Primary School, Hull

Ava Catherine Coulson (9)	5
Addison Jones (11)	6
Emma Rose Skerrett (10)	8
Amy Louise Tomlinson (10)	10
Farah Mann (10)	11
Amelie Abramson (7)	12
Ava Kleinhout (10)	13
Lilly Hustwait (9)	14

Kingswood Parks Primary School, Kingswood

Annabel May Snowden (8)	15
Esther Baldwin (10)	16
Theo Draper (11)	18
Lauren Marris (8)	21
Rebecca Hesp (7)	22
Libby Wilson (8)	24
Annabelle Rose Sedgwick (7)	26
Maddison Grace Cox (10)	28
Harry Middleton (10)	30
Blake Scott (7)	32
Archie Steven Ellam (10)	34
Charlie Stretton (10)	36
Poppy Hirst (8)	38
Cameron Carter (8)	40
Charlie Holdstock (8)	41
Evie Colton (7)	42

Olivia Jowett (10)	43
Macie-Lou Stonell (8)	44
Emily Chapman (8)	45
Isaac Wright (7)	46
Aiden Houston (7)	47
Joe Rose (10)	48
Mia Sollitt (8)	50
Jack Young (9)	51
Poppy Rose Beal (7)	52
Tyler Jake Hannath (10)	53
Ellie Simmester (8)	54
Lily Hoyle (8)	55
Ruby Cross (10)	56
Jacob Washbrook (9)	57
Emily Miller (8)	58
Mason Jon Kirby (9)	59
Benjamin Rhys Cornelius (9)	60
Seth Isaac Rock (8)	61
Emillie Carroll (9)	62
Lewis Smith (8)	63
Aaron Eastwood (7)	64
Ava Garmston (7)	65
Megan Dunn (7)	66
Luke Marris (9)	67
Jack David Bolton (7)	68
Thomas Peden (9)	69
Kaira Simmons (9)	70
Grace Pollard (9)	71
Liam Shepherdson (10)	72
Evelyn Drinkall (9)	73
Riley Steven Wilson (9)	74
Sophie Hopkins (9)	75
Lillian Shakira Hamilton (11)	76
Harry Wakefield (9)	77
Elisha-Joy Baldwin (8)	78

Rhys Harrison (8)	79
Alfie Samson (10)	80
Theodore Jones (7)	81
Ava Barley (8)	82
Ellie-Rose Albrow (9)	84
Jack Drinkall (9)	85
Roma Valentino Hird (9)	86
Amelia Rose Ainley (10)	87
Satya Hasini Giri (7)	88
Sofie Marie Goralora (9)	89
Imogen Sophia Jefferson (9)	90
Aimee Mae Green (9)	91
Olivia Brockbank (8)	92
Evie Jo Ellam (7)	93
Elissia Grace Brown (10)	94
Amelia Wisniewska (7)	95
Rima Saeed Alshahrani (8)	96
Gabbie Jane McDonald (10)	97
Ellie May Woods (8)	98
Grace Dinsdale (10)	99
Ethan Turner (7)	100
Faris Alghamdi (9)	101
Alex Waller (7)	102
Oliver Smith (10)	103
Billy Drury (9)	104
Amelia Spicer-Matthews (9)	105
Harley Marshall (10)	106
Isabelle Marie Fellows (8)	107
Lola Drury (9)	108
Benjamin Hopkins (8)	109
Dylan Harry Booker-Kingdom (8)	110
Angelina Ferriby (9)	111
Elliott Robinson (9)	112
Charlie Stanley Waudby (8)	113
Freddie Reuben Jessop (8)	114
Eva Brooks (8)	115
Seth Whittaker (8)	116
Oliver Henley (9)	117
Lucas Lamplough (7)	118
Scarlett Azelia Taylor (8)	119
Chloe Chapman (8)	120
Megan Johnson (10)	121

Maybury Primary School, Hull

Holly Casey (10)	122
Destynie Monkman (9)	123
Phoebe-Mai Jenkins (9)	124
Ella Dockerty (11)	125
Olivia May Hardy (9)	126

Newington Academy, Hull

Alan Drewno (9)	127
Savanna Thompson (9)	128
Lenny Jones (9)	129
George Leason (9)	130
Simona Tina Vacmane (9)	131
Julia Bartczak (9)	132
Amber Scaum (9)	133
Wiktor Skorupa (9)	134
Ben Leeman (9)	135
Nataniel Zoch (10)	136
Mackennya Wilkinson (9)	137
Mason Jameson (10)	138
Oliwia Styga (10)	139
Matthew James Bateman (9)	140
Alexa Simpson (9)	141
Charlie James Kennedy (9)	142

St Andrew's CE Primary School, Sutton Park

Farren Roper (10)	143
Ellie Walker (11)	144
Jasmine Molloy (10)	146
Elicia JLJ Spivey (10)	147
Andrew Opene (10)	148
Harry Moon (10)	149
Olivia Christine Fullard (10)	150
Emily Myers (10)	151
Samuel Paul Jordan (10)	152
Harlie (10) & Grace McKenzie	153
Harry Busby (10)	154
Ruby Grace Agnew (10)	156
Dylan Smith (10)	158
Graicee-Ella Caulfield (10)	159

Adam Taylor (10)	160
Callum Barley (10)	161
Codie Hewick (11)	162
Harry Rudkin (10)	163
Millie Jane Stewart (10)	164
Alex Tarsey (10)	165
Ava Grace Pearson (10)	166
Connor David Vass (10)	167
Lauren Longley (10)	168
Lily Elizabeth Emma Russell (10)	169
Oscar Jools Foley (10)	170
Poppy Blanchard (10)	171
Kaiden Riley (10)	172
Alexis Bottomley (10)	173
Evie Grace Hussey (10)	174
William Talbot (10) & Jay Logan Johnson	175
Harris Chapman (10)	176
Myles Alan Micheal McCloud (10)	177
Alfie Brennan (10)	178
Joshua Horne (10)	179
Megan Hall (10)	180
Reuben Hawkes (10)	181
Mia Violet Lydon (11) & Mia-Ren	182
Lily Bunby (10)	183
Archie Quest (10)	184
Evie-Louise Jay (10)	185
Jaidyn Foster (10)	186
Breanna Leigh Johnson (10)	187
Holly Richardson (10)	188
Alex McNamara (10)	189
Jay Keal (10)	190
Jack Dunn (11)	191
Rio Kassim (10)	192
Finlay Jaydon Mortimer (10)	193
William Wilson (10)	194

Stoneferry Primary School, Hull

Harris Adamson (10)	195
Jessica Meara (10)	196
Jake Peter Goforth (10)	198
James Bailey (10)	199
Bradley Corran (10)	200
Leonardo de Castro Ferreira (10)	201
Brett Craig (10)	202
Alfie Wadsworth (10)	203
Victoria Payne (10)	204
Joshua Lee Stonehouse (10)	205
Tyler Wadsworth (10)	206
Megan Rose Taylor (10)	207
Riley Robert Pearce (10)	208
Ema Sava (10)	209

The Poems

A Mysterious Land

Down the rabbit hole, down, down,
Down, down, down,
Ears popping,
All you see is brown.

Suddenly you're there,
A wonderland,
You see a hare,
It isn't so bland.

You see a cockroach singing,
As beautifully as can be,
Dancing marmalade,
And an odd melody.

Further in you see,
A forest so beautiful, so bold,
An old merchant,
Whose merch has been sold.

You continue on and meet,
A fairy named Silky,
Who is as sweet as honey,

A chap named Moon-Face,
Who really loves toffee.

A guy called the Saucepan Man,
With his shop hanging,
He prefers honey,
And Mr Waziname,
Whose real name is a mystery.

Wave goodbye for now,
You need to leave,
Goodbye, goodbye,
We'll see you next time!

Christine Hua Vong (10)
Broadacre Primary School, Hull

Is It All A Dream?

My name is Ruby, I'm ever so curious, just you wait and see,
For it is me loving every moment,
I see a hole deep in the ground, my curiosity grows,
I take one step and off I go!
What I see is a magical tree calling me, "Ruby!"
I swim to the tree, wonder fills my mind,
As I climb the ladder of mystery!
Without hesitation, I go through the door,
Filled with unicorns, bicorns and tricorns, plus aliens,
Believe it or not, there are more and more,
Oh no, oh dear me, curse my curiosity,
But as time flies by me,
The others get on and become friends,
I close my eyes with hope and ask someone to pinch me,
And surely, just as she does,
A magic sparkly cloud comes over me,
As I open my eyes, I see my comfy bed,
My snuggly ted and I slide myself into bed,
At this moment, my mummy comes in,

To read me my bedtime story,
I never think it's a boring story that'll make me snorey,
Zzzz! Just as Mummy leaves the room,
I start to wonder what is that great big thunder,
So I shake my head and nod off to bed,
Back to Dreamland on my favourite rocket ship with my trusty ted.

Ruby Jay Scarah (10)
Broadacre Primary School, Hull

Inside Technology

One minute I was in my bed asleep,
Although before I knew it, I had taken a leap,
Into what must have been technology,
Even though it was great, I had wires around me,
I could see all the levels from my games,
Even all of the characters and their names,
Suddenly I pressed a button, then I was gone,
I saw the newsreader talking about a con,
I was flying through the internet, colours and sounds zooming past,
I felt rather dizzy, I was going so fast,
Below me I saw Facebook, Google and Twitter,
I was sure I'd just seen a Pokémon critter,
Next, I saw YouTube videos flashing by,
Ohh, there went Joe Sugg, I had to wave hi,
Interesting facts whizzed on by,
Egyptians and their camels, how amazing, oh my,
A puff of smoke and a pop,
With a jump and a hop,
I came out of the screen,
And back into my dream!

Ava Catherine Coulson (9)
Cottingham Croxby Primary School, Hull

Candy Wonderland!

I opened my eyes,
Just to see,
The wonderful world,
Surrounding me.

Rushing rivers of custard,
Gummy bears on a tree,
Houses made of chocolate,
With a gingerbread key.

How had I got to that wonderland?
It was a big mystery,
But I took one look around,
And knew there was nowhere better to be.

I ran to a fountain,
A grin on my face,
The dripping milk chocolate,
Made my heart start to race.

I heard rustling in the bushes,
Which was made by chocolate mice,

They scared me very badly,
So they'd have to pay the price.

After my big filling feast,
Around Candyland I decided to roam,
And after that, I lay down to nap,
But when I awoke I was home.

Addison Jones (11)
Cottingham Croxby Primary School, Hull

The Fun-Filled, Action-Packed Paradise!

Open your eyes to a mystical land,
With boisterous butterflies as small as grains of sand,
Monstrous, monumental, murky mountains,
And lethal lava spewing out of fountains,
Fantasy forests filled with flaming phoenixes and dazzling dragons,
And fabulous fireballs fired from cannons,
Twisting, twirling trees turn and dance,
As the luscious leaves leap and prance,
The caves packed full of delicious adventures,
Go inside if you dare to venture,
Mint Jujubes and cherry tubes,
Luminous lollies and passion fruit jollies,
Everlasting gobstoppers and never-blasting bogtrotters,
It's a flavour-filled fairground,
Chocolate rivers *splash, splash!* What a wonderful sound,
Cookie spaceships,

And houses of chips,
It's a magical paradise,
So jump in and take a slice!

Emma Rose Skerrett (10)
Cottingham Croxby Primary School, Hull

Candy Wonderland

Welcome, welcome to Candy Wonderland,
Anything you wish for is at our command.
From all things sweet, to all things sour,
We have plenty of goodies for you to devour.

There's a gingerbread house and gummy bear tree,
Anything you choose will bring lots of glee.
Go on, pick something, take what you want,
Then sit and enjoy it in our fancy restaurant.

If you like chocolate, check out the waterfall,
Anything you desire, we have it all.
The lovely, luscious lollipops taste great to eat,
The mouthwatering milkshakes cannot be beat.

Candyfloss clouds, chocolate drop rain,
Anything tasty like sweet sugar cane.
Don't get too greedy, remember to share,
Enjoy smelling warm melted chocolate in the air.

Amy Louise Tomlinson (10)
Cottingham Croxby Primary School, Hull

Mythical Land

Mist, cries, laughter, I hear all around me,
Screams, cries, laughter are all I can hear in this mythical land,
Creatures shouting and screeching,
It's not very appealing,
It is a war zone, no one can help,
Werewolves howling,
It helps when I read a book from JK Rowling,
Whilst prowling up and down,
I see a llama which is very fortunate,
Because my mamma wants a llama,
Now it's time to go back home,
Which means I have to pay off the loan.

Farah Mann (10)
Cottingham Croxby Primary School, Hull

Candy Land

C andyfloss clouds are fluffy
A ll pink and blue
N ear the ground are sugar trees that grow up to the clouds
D ropping from the clouds, it's raining Skittles and Rainbow Drops
Y ummy chocolate water fountains.

L akes made of custard
A re perfect for swimming
N ext to the lake sits a palace made out of sugar crystals
D uring the sun, the marshmallow, gingerbread roofs lie on top of the walls.

Amelie Abramson (7)
Cottingham Croxby Primary School, Hull

The Candy Land

I looked outside my window to see,
Red and white candy cane trees,
Chocolate lakes and cocoa falls,
And Smartie stepping stones,
Swirly lollipop roses,
Sugar paper grass,
And a kingdom of jelly beans!
My mum called and said it was tea,
It was vegetable soup again for me.

Ava Kleinhout (10)
Cottingham Croxby Primary School, Hull

Dragon Dream

I can see the bright red lava scales,
I can smell smoke engulfing the trees in seconds,
I can touch the smooth, warm eggs falling off the dragon tree,
I can hear the roar of gigantic dragons,
I can taste the wonderful taste of ripe peach on my tongue,
I feel amazing,
What can you feel?

Lilly Hustwait (9)
Cottingham Croxby Primary School, Hull

Our Street

Our street is a magical place

Say unicorns on rainbows,
talking cats, rainbow dogs.
Our street is a crazy place

Say singing ladybirds,
spotty houses, cheesy moons.
Our street is a loud place

Say screeching birds,
shouting kids, singing statues.
Our street is a new place

Say shining roofs,
clean paths, glittering shops.
Our street is not a normal place

Say unicorns on rainbows,
singing ladybirds and a cheesy moon.
But my street is the best.

Says me!

Annabel May Snowden (8)
Kingswood Parks Primary School, Kingswood

Survival Of The Clever

It feels so isolated down here,
Trying to get people to notice me,
The trees so vast and the twigs so miniscule,
The empty hollow place towering over me.

Searching like a wolf for its prey,
I look for twigs for my SOS sign,
(Wanting to hold onto my life),
Dodge the trees.

Hands stepping forwards,
Grabbing the logs to make my shelter,
Dream-deep concentration fills me,
Foretelling every second of the way to survival.

Raise arms,
Quickly step forwards,
Look up slowly and duck down,
Watching for any logs falling down from the sky.

Rolling the logs down the hill,
My sweat-filled head crying for help,
Desperate to have a shelter,

I climb up the trees,
And grab leaves to cover my only home.

Hands torn,
The logs just balanced,
I look into my shelter,
All alone and wet,
There is nobody but me.

Esther Baldwin (10)
Kingswood Parks Primary School, Kingswood

A Raft Of Emotions

It feels terrifying sat here,
On the uncomfortable, shaking seat,
And the everlasting blue lake so close by.

Stretch to the left,
Pull my foot towards me and gently,
(Holding onto the cold rubber paddle like the last breath in the world)
Climb onto the raft.

Arms down,
Slowly facing the front,
Shoulders relaxed,
Silent passion,
Rope tight as a crowd appear behind me,
Ready to push the raft into the deep blue lake.

All of a sudden,
Wood starts to move,
The barrels squeak like an angry mouse,
The raft hangs off the edge,
Ready for take off.

Plunge into the water,
Almost sinking,
Then, *snap!*
The raft falls into two pieces,
The barrels float away into the distance,
1000 faces giggling at the same time,
Then at the last second,
I paddle to the edge.

Clunk!
The barrels hit against the side,
One slips on,
Two step on,
My feet feel relieved to be on ground,
As they clutch the cold, muddy water,
Then, *Splash!*
One of my companions falls into the water,
My instinct instinctively makes me go to help him.

I pull and pull till my feet lose grip and I fall in,
Darkness consumes me as all I can see is black,
But as I think this is the end,
I appear above the water.

Arms still,
Fingers straight,
Forwards, cutting the blue skin of the water,
Finally, I reach the end,
Get back up and walk away with a dripping, cold body.

Theo Draper (11)
Kingswood Parks Primary School, Kingswood

This World

This world isn't a boring place

Say the mystical flying
alicorns and magical
unicorns

This world isn't based on school

Say the loud and
amazing parties
overnight and even during the mornings

This world isn't a normal place

Say the dancing horses and
the alicorns doing
gymnastics, even Pegasus doing the splits in the air!

This world isn't a green place

Say the candy wrappers on the floor and melted chocolate on the grass

Says me!

Lauren Marris (8)
Kingswood Parks Primary School, Kingswood

Our Street

Our street is a green place,

Say the tall trees, lush green bushes and soft grass.

Our street is a tidy place,

Say the full clean bins, well cared for gardens and beautiful clean cars.

Our street is not a new place,

Say the old dirty bricks, grey driveways and wooden fences.

Our street is not a short one,

Say the long roads, long driveways and long green fields.

Our street is a quiet place,

Say the chirping birds, quiet people and the slow opening doors.

Our street is not a posh place,

Say the cheap cars, kids in shorts and the cheap houses.

Our street is not a lazy place,

Say the wide-awake people, busy children and hunting animals.

But our street is the best,
Says me!

Rebecca Hesp (7)
Kingswood Parks Primary School, Kingswood

My Adventure In Cookie Land

When I awoke,
I was in a different world,
I looked outside at the hut,
To see what I had woken up in.

Outside I saw a door,
Oh so very poor,
Chocolate chips, oh so yummy,
All in my big tummy.

My eyes were blurred by the chocolate river,
And chocolate fountain that ran down the road,
Oh so yummy it could be funny.

Walking down the chocolate road,
Meeting a chocolate toad,
Wanting to eat him,
But no, no, no because he was too cute,
To go in my big tummy.

Reaching the end of the chocolate road,

I saw a whole school of toads,
Oh there were so many,
Maybe just one in my tummy.

Yummy, yummy in my tummy,
All in one, I gulped down the chocolate toad,
And disappeared up the chocolate road.

Libby Wilson (8)
Kingswood Parks Primary School, Kingswood

Our Street

Our street is a green place,
Say the freshly mowed hills, brown wavy trees,
And the cared for gardens.

Our street is a flowery street,
Say the yellow roses, beautiful tulips,
And the three-leaf clovers.

Our street is a sleepy place,
Say the sleeping children in bed, tired babies,
And the snoozing mums and dads.

Our street is sometimes a tidy place,
Say the empty Capri-Suns, half-filled bins,
And the wriggly pink worms.

Our street is a cool place,
Say the posh Mitsubishi cars, the blue Co-op,
And the pharmacy.

Our street is a peaceful place,
Say the white fluttering butterflies, tweeting birds,
And buzzing bees.

Our street is a short place,
Say the Royal Mail postmen and the old clothes pick up men,
But our street is the best says me!

Annabelle Rose Sedgwick (7)
Kingswood Parks Primary School, Kingswood

Cold Swim

It feels very cold in here,
Against the slippery, wet fish,
The raft so far away,
Tied in the figure eight knot,
1000 smiling faces.

Swimming in the fish-filled lake,
(Scrunched feet, as a smooth thing slithers past my iced flesh),
Facing a ripple,
Squelchy feet.

Raise my legs slowly up and down,
An ocean of rocks colliding with my luscious skin,
Every second of the coming paddle.

Then, with a sudden downwards temperature,
The lake turns into negatives,
Feet like flippers,
Gathering speed to splash to the very successful raft.

At the last split second,
The strong water pulls the raft.

The flesh of the lake is chopped in half,
By the power of my needle-sharp hands,
The raft swims back to shore,
We are ready for our final jump...

Maddison Grace Cox (10)
Kingswood Parks Primary School, Kingswood

Fast Drive!

It feels terrifying,
Crouched here on the lumpy, vibrating seat,
Mountains of engines so close to my body!

Stumble to the left,
Push a foot and now stop in excitement,
(Hold the scaly, cold handlebars)
Move up on the quad bike.

Raise arms slowly, sideways,
The revs are climbing silently,
Light on face, concentration,
Every second is a coming fight.

Then with a sudden upward beat of roaring sound,
Like a person gathering more speed,
I lurch forwards,
Take off around the track.

Roll to a quadruple rev,
That at that spilt second takes off like an angry person.

Nerves turning as I pray,
Not followed,
Bones stab the wind like an eagle plunging,
Deep into the corner without a crash.

Harry Middleton (10)
Kingswood Parks Primary School, Kingswood

Our Street

Our street is a posh place,

Say all the nans taking the bins out, the mums and dads going to work in their expensive posh cars and all of the kind beautiful school children.

Our street is a quiet place,

Say all the snoozing cats, the careful window cleaner and the special mailman.

Our street is a tidy place,

Say the careful binmen, say all the careful people who put it in the black, blue and brown bins and the strong and careful window cleaner.

Our street is not a lazy place,

Says the careful window cleaner, the speedy bike rider and the quick bush cutter who cuts the huge bushes.

Our street is a short place,

Say all the kind people who live there, the Asda man and the children who walk home from school.

But our street is the best,
Says me.

Blake Scott (7)
Kingswood Parks Primary School, Kingswood

Blinded Senses!

It felt very tense under the dingy,
Unlit goggles,
Blindfolded,
Waiting to find out what I could be facing next,
The sound of tweeting birds consumed me.

Face a blank wall,
The leaves crunched under my feet
Blood ran through my veins,
Butterflies were fluttering around my stomach.

My hand burned as it ran across the rough, snake-like rope,
Travelling through the serene forest,
Laughter lifted my jaw.

Bones rested on my shoulders,
My feet banged onto a rubbery circle,
My heart skipped a beat,
Screams congested me.

Whack!

My head hit a wooden wall,
The sensory trail was done.

Archie Steven Ellam (10)
Kingswood Parks Primary School, Kingswood

PGL In Space

Exciting, in the rocket and on to the moon,
The alien instructor sat us down to tell us what we were doing,
We were told that our first activity was space shooting,
The aliens were watching,
Us shooting creatures,
We were also asteroid jumping,
But not too high,
The asteroids were big,
Just like all of space,
All there was to hear,
Was the sun burning from 1000 miles away,
We woke up on fluffy, soft clouds,
Which were so see-through,
Most of the time, there were spaceships rattling past,
In never-ending space,
We had been building hover cars,
With the hard, grey moon rock,
Walking along the plain white clouds,

We glided down to our activity point,
To end the blessed PGL in space trip.

Charlie Stretton (10)
Kingswood Parks Primary School, Kingswood

The Science Lab

We left the school,
As quiet as mice,
You could hear a pin drop,
As we walked to the academy with pride.

We were finally there,
We walked as proud as lions,
Through the academy,
As everyone stared in astonishment.

Lining up,
Ready to go in,
Jumping around like kangaroos,
Suddenly, he opened the door and we all ran inside...

Making bubbling slime,
Experimenting, dissolving,
Having lots of fun,
With everyone!

Then it was finished,
It was time to go back,

But we had a great time,
At the science lab!

Poppy Hirst (8)
Kingswood Parks Primary School, Kingswood

Kingswood

Our street is quite a posh place,

Say the mums in dresses,
Dads in suits,
Kids in school wear.
Our street is a quiet place,

Say our football matches,
Our squeaking bikes,
Our calls.
Our street is a pretty tidy place,

Say the lolly wrappers,
Falling food,
And broken cars.
Our street is not a small place,

Say the car washing dads,
Clothes washing mums,
And smart boys.
Our street is not a short one,

But our street is the best,
Say us!

Cameron Carter (8)
Kingswood Parks Primary School, Kingswood

Our Street

Our street is a posh place

Says pizza man Jeff,
Jim the builder, Asda man Lee,
Our street is a brand new place

Say the working dads,
Tidying mums and playing boys,
Our street is a ginormous one

Say the mums in dresses,
Dads in suits and kids in school uniforms,
Our street is a silent place

Say the marshmallows falling like rain,
Dragons in the garden,
Houses made out of jelly beans and chocolate
Our street is the best

Says me!

Our street has changed!

Charlie Holdstock (8)
Kingswood Parks Primary School, Kingswood

Our Street

Our street is a green place,

Say the green leaves on the trees, the red roses and the light blue flowering bushes.

Our street is not a new place,

Say the holey concrete on the walls, the broken bricks on the floor and the broken, cracked tree trunks.

Our street is a posh place,

Say shiny, posh cars, the shimmering leaves and the clear, sparkling glass on the houses.

Our street is not a quiet place,

Say the bright brown woodpeckers, the black owls and the tweeting birds.

But our street is the best,

Says me!

Evie Colton (7)
Kingswood Parks Primary School, Kingswood

Planet Moon

Today was the day,
The day we were going to Planet Moon,
Pulling the tight spacesuit up my body,
Fastening the zip and buttons,
The oxygen tank on my back, heavy but needed,
The two year six classes pranced to the spaceship,
Up, up! Off we went!
We soared through the blue sunny skies,
After a while, through the small strong windows,
We saw the galaxy appear in the distance,
Golden stars lit up while the rocket ship landed,
We dismounted and a few of us fell into the craters,
We all leapt onto hover bikes as soon as we saw them,
We drove hover bikes up and down!
We drove all the way around the moon -
Even upside down!

Olivia Jowett (10)
Kingswood Parks Primary School, Kingswood

My Terrible Street

My street is terrible,
Say the mums in big fluffy jackets,
Dads in humongous coats, kids in colourful caps,
This street isn't a nice place.

Say our barking dogs, our plain broken bikes, our screams,
Our street is a bad place.

Says the glass on the floor, rubbish on the floor,
And graffiti on the walls.

This street isn't a nice place for football,
Say the shouting dads,
Upset mums and annoying boys.

Our street isn't so bad,
Cute wild cats roaming on the streets,
I love my street.

Macie-Lou Stonell (8)
Kingswood Parks Primary School, Kingswood

Our Busy Street

Our street is a posh place

Say the kids throwing cakes at Mum's dress

Our street is a quiet place

Say our football matches
And our clown horns

Our street is a tidy place

Say the lolly wrappers,
Chippy and written on walls

Our street is not a lazy place

Say the dads getting wet from water bombs
While washing the cars
And mums getting wet
While washing clothes

My street is the best!

Emily Chapman (8)
Kingswood Parks Primary School, Kingswood

Our Street

Our street is a tidy place,
Say the clean bins, smooth paths and freshly polished cars.

Our street is a very green street,
Say the rose bushes, the lovely flower beds and the spiky palm trees.

Our street is a new place,
Say the new bricks, the fresh paint on the doors and the new glass for the window panes.

Our street is a posh place,
Say the expensive cars, expensive houses and lovely gardens.

Our street is a quiet street,
Say the silent children, silent mums and silent dads.

But our street is the best,
Says me.

Isaac Wright (7)
Kingswood Parks Primary School, Kingswood

Our Street

Our street is a tidy place,

Say the mirror-like cars, the freshly-cut grass and all the rubbish in bins.

Our street is an expensive place,

Say the shiny Lamborghinis, modern Peugeots and £1000 mansions.

My street is a fashionable place,

Say the kids in Nike trackies with holes in, teenagers in skinny jeans and parents in white suits.

Our street is not a quiet place,

Say the kids playing out, people playing tag and kids screaming.

But our street is the best,
Says me!

Aiden Houston (7)
Kingswood Parks Primary School, Kingswood

Soaking Secrets...

Down the tall hill,
Spotting the enormous barrels,
Feeling frightened,
Near the area of the camp,
So high up,
Thousands of hungry carps,
Waiting to ravenously devour human flesh.

Walking to the half-made vehicle,
(Tight hands on a rope)
Hanging on to the last hold of land.

Leg stepping on,
Then my other leg,
Then bum shuffling,
On the end, our courageous squad,
Staring at the murky lake,
Who knows what's in there?

Then suddenly, wobbling like an old pirate ship,
The bodies shaking in fear,
Then a sudden slip,
Darkness in the water,

Launching up like a nuclear missile,
Air at last.

Pushing against the thick mud,
Sailing away,
I swim,
Grabbing onto the shore.

Arms pointed,
I am scared,
Being dragged out,
Flopping like a fish to catch air,
Then I see a much bigger shadow in the lake,
What is it?

Joe Rose (10)
Kingswood Parks Primary School, Kingswood

Our Street

Our street is an amazingly posh place.

Say the mums in dresses,
Dads in suits,
Kids in school wear.

Our street is a lovely quiet place.

Say our school matches,
Our fashionable bikes,
The fun that comes out.

Our street is a lovely tidy place.

Say the chattering Christmas trees,
Speeding bikes,
And healthy food that we eat.

Written on walls, lovely art.

Our street is not a lazy place.

Mia Sollitt (8)
Kingswood Parks Primary School, Kingswood

The Day Of The Fun Run

Today was the day, I stood at the starting line,
As my nerves dragged me back,
As I was getting cheered on,
My body lost some of my nerves.

As pain came to my legs,
My legs felt like they were dreaming,
My legs crossed the finish line,
I felt like I was dead.

I was as proud as the first man on the moon,
When I finished, I was already a winner,
I helped my friends finish the race,
As pride dived through me.

After the day of proudness,
The day of nervousness,
My body felt numb.

Jack Young (9)
Kingswood Parks Primary School, Kingswood

Our Street

Our street is not a lazy place because we like adventures,

Say the mums in bows, the dads in hats and the children in headphones and shorts.

Our street is calm,

Says the ice lolly man and the hot dog man.

Our street is a green place,

Say the leafy beautiful trees and the really nice rose bushes.

Our street is old,

Say the crumbly dirty walls and really old houses.

Our street is clean,

Say all the empty Coca-Cola cans in the bin.

Poppy Rose Beal (7)
Kingswood Parks Primary School, Kingswood

Higher You Go, Faster You Fall

Climb, climb, climb, fall, fall, fall
Into an endless pit of
darkness and terror.

Can't go down so go up!
A blue line of terror
waiting to be unleashed.

A million eyes watch
A tower as tall as a skyscraper
and as enormous as King Kong.

People fall, cry and all
As soon as they pass
the line.

People try, don't succeed
Endless anger and terror
Coming to see
the beautiful bell.

Tyler Jake Hannath (10)
Kingswood Parks Primary School, Kingswood

My Special Street

Our street is totally a posh place,
Say the mums who cook, the dads with perfect teeth,
Our street is a
Perfect place.

See us cooperating as a team,
Our street is
A warming, comfy
Place.

See us not littering we
Put our bags in the bin,
Today we recycle
Our litter,
We have no graffiti on walls.

See mums that have babies,
Playful boys and girls,
Our street is a comfy place,
Says me!

Ellie Simmester (8)
Kingswood Parks Primary School, Kingswood

My Precious Street

Our street is posh,
From the raining marshmallows we eat,
Our street is tidy,
That means we recycle,
Our street is peaceful,
Our pavements are made out of trampolines,
So we bounce when we walk.

When we walk we chew,
The most chewiest gum,
Shooting from the sky,
We are so rich,
Because money grows on trees.

We are getting famous,
Because we're meeting famous people,
Like Hollywood actresses,
We're going to become movie stars.

Lily Hoyle (8)
Kingswood Parks Primary School, Kingswood

The Plane Journey

Turbulence,
Wobble,
Crash,
In the air, it was like a dream,
We were gliding through the clouds,
But I was sort of missing my family.

Turbulence,
Wobble,
Crash,
Eight hours left,
One hour passed and I was bored,
Six,
Five,
Four,
I was still waiting.

Three hours later, there came a big bang,
We landed, we landed in America,
But in the sky, my journey had only just started.

Ruby Cross (10)
Kingswood Parks Primary School, Kingswood

Fun Run

The line was drawn.
Excitement made me pumped for the race.
Eyes hung upon me.
The coach shouted, "One!"

I legged it.
One, two, how many people?
I started to slow down,
But determination kept me going.

I felt like jelly.
I was way ahead.
The finish line was mine.

At the last second...
I was overtaken,
But I was still proud.
I felt like I was going to faint.
Second was my place.

Jacob Washbrook (9)
Kingswood Parks Primary School, Kingswood

Candy Land

Welcome to Candy Land,
My street is in Candy Land,
You can meet me there.

On my street, there is a pool,
Made out of jelly and Nutella,
Pools are amazing here.

When you stay, where you stay,
Is made out of cookies,
And you can play as long as you want to.

You can sit on sugar lumps,
And watch ladybirds sing.

I can feel jelly beans on the floor,
I like my home.

Welcome to Candy Land.

Emily Miller (8)
Kingswood Parks Primary School, Kingswood

The Big Goal

I was stood at the starting line
The crowd made me nervous
My heart started to pound like a drum
The crowd watched.

As the man counted down
I already felt like giving up
But I knew there wasn't time.

I began to run
I was determined to win
I ran like a cheetah chasing the finish
I would not let anyone in front of me.

I ran to the finish line
My legs were like jelly
But I made it eventually.

Mason Jon Kirby (9)
Kingswood Parks Primary School, Kingswood

The Run

The day of the run.
Worry was acid burning my hopes
Would I cross the line?
Who knew?
Yet I was still a man.

I rooted my feet to the dominating line.
Fear came!
It was like the devil revealing his crooked
dagger, then thrusting it into my soul,
my guts spilling everywhere.

There I was near the end,
flying like a blazing phoenix.
I did it!
Happiness!
I faced my fears and so should you.

Benjamin Rhys Cornelius (9)
Kingswood Parks Primary School, Kingswood

My World

My world is a peaceful place
not a loud place, it
is green and orange and blue.

My world is
not a normal place
but an
imaginary
place.

My world is not
a tiny place
says the vast skate park
and the titanic gardens.

My world
is my most
perfect world
ever.

Says me!

Seth Isaac Rock (8)
Kingswood Parks Primary School, Kingswood

The Race Day

The day of the race came
My heart was pounding like a lion about to roar
Stepping back, a shiver fell down my spine
The whistle blew - no turning back.

Chanting names as the finish line got further away
Feeling like jelly
Sprinting fast
But representing Kingswood Parks.

Panting like a dog
A smile hit my face
Not feeling anything but joy.

Didn't get first place,
But to me it was first place.

Emillie Carroll (9)
Kingswood Parks Primary School, Kingswood

My House

My house is a busy place,

Say the animals upstairs and
the pool in my room.

My house is a big place,

Says the boat in my loft,
and the long grass in the backyard.

My house is a crazy place,

Like the cows mooing in the backyard,
and the chickens laying eggs.

My house is the best,

Says me!

Lewis Smith (8)
Kingswood Parks Primary School, Kingswood

Our Street

Our street is a very green place,

Says the soft grass, lush green bushes and freshly mowed hills.

Our street is not a posh place,

Say the fallen over rubbish bins, the gardens covered in weeds and the children's dirty clothes.

Our street is a quiet place,

Say the sleeping dogs, the snoozing babies and mummies watching quiet movies.

But our street is the best,

Says me!

Aaron Eastwood (7)
Kingswood Parks Primary School, Kingswood

Our Street

Our street is a tidy place,

Say the clean bins, beautiful big houses and the green prickly bushes.

Our street is a posh place,

Say the beautiful flowers, the shiny golden cars and the big tall houses.

Our street is a quiet place,

Say the quiet small cars, the old brown dogs and the quiet people in the cold early morning air.

Our street is the best,

Says me!

Ava Garmston (7)
Kingswood Parks Primary School, Kingswood

Our Street

My street is beautiful and green.
Also my street has beautiful trees.
Our street is a posh place to live.
Our street is a new place.
Our street is the best.
Our street is a tidy place to live.
Our street is a lovely place.
Our street is cool.
Our street has lots of houses.

Our street has beautiful flowers.
Our street is wonderful.

But our street is the best,
Says me!

Megan Dunn (7)
Kingswood Parks Primary School, Kingswood

The Fun Run

The day of the fun run.
Determination was a coach,
Coaching me every step of the way.
Might I reach the finish line?

Standing halfway across the course, I lost determination.
Fear entered me.
I was a mouse and fear was choosing me.
Was this the way to get me moving?

Crossing the finish line, I felt victorious.
My legs were shaking.
My eyes were watering.
I was more amazed than anything!

Luke Marris (9)
Kingswood Parks Primary School, Kingswood

Our Street

Our street is a green place,

Say the beautiful gardens, shiny polished cars and the lush wavy grass.

Our street is a tidy place,

Say the full dirty bins, smooth clean concrete and caring binmen.

Our street is not a short one,

Say the long muddy car trails, yellow and red cars and lots of dirty old drives.

But our street is the best,

Says me!

Jack David Bolton (7)
Kingswood Parks Primary School, Kingswood

Fun Run Worry

The day of the fun run.
Worry was like a clock rolling
at the same time as I was running.
Would I be able to cross
the finish line?

As the nerves got to me
I felt like the finish line was
waiting for me.
Was my destiny first or last place?

Crossing the finish line was like a
train hitting my body
with relief.
I couldn't believe I had done it.

Thomas Peden (9)
Kingswood Parks Primary School, Kingswood

Fun Run Day

The day of the fun run
Worried as a cat
Seeking around my stomach
Will I get to the finish line in time?

Standing on the horrid starting line
Fear is a lightning strike
Will I come in last place or not?

Crossing the finish line
Relief spans and drifts around me
Like a person holding a red flag, a bull chasing
My prize is my trophy which is gold
I will never forget this day.

Kaira Simmons (9)
Kingswood Parks Primary School, Kingswood

The Day Of The Tummy Bug

The day of the tummy bug
Worry was a thunderstorm rumbling in my stomach
Was I really getting a stomach bug?

Sitting in bed, I felt weird
Vomiting felt melancholy
My mum came racing like lightning up the stairs
Would I have to stay off school?

Stumbling to the doctors
I was a clock tick-tocking with fear
Shivering, I went step by step into the doctors
Would it be something to worry about?

Grace Pollard (9)
Kingswood Parks Primary School, Kingswood

The Fun Run

The day of the fun run.
Worry was like a weight pulling me down,
Would I ever reach the long-awaited finish line?

On the starting line.
Fear was a lightning strike burning my body.
I was scared of coming last.
Was I losing my only hope?

Crossing the finish line.
Pride filled my body, all the other emotions poured out.
Sprinting as fast as I could.
Pride was my golden ticket into Heaven.

Liam Shepherdson (10)
Kingswood Parks Primary School, Kingswood

Fantastic Fun Run Day

I stood at the starting line,
Nervousness stalked through the crowds that didn't see him,
Shaking like a jelly, I took my place,
Bang! I was going for first place.

I went round the second bend,
I was like a cheetah chasing its prey,
But my prey was the finish line,
Determination sprinted past the last bend to the finish line.

My legs felt like jelly again,
I was almost at the end,
I crossed the line,
Tiredness lay on the floor as nobody noticed him.

I was as proud as a peacock,
As proud as a lion,
Proudness stood on the first place block as he had pictures taken of him,
It really was a fantastic fun run day.

Evelyn Drinkall (9)
Kingswood Parks Primary School, Kingswood

The Day Of The Fun Run

Nerves, excitement, dread
My heart sprinted like a rapid cheetah
The whistle blew!
My legs pulled me forwards like somebody was pushing me

I ran
My legs felt like jelly
I felt proud
I was guaranteed to win

I dashed from my predator
My legs dragged me there
"Don't give up now!"
I had pride in everything I did.

Riley Steven Wilson (9)
Kingswood Parks Primary School, Kingswood

River Walk

The day of the river walk
Excitement was a butterfly
Fluttering around my thought-filled mind
Why did I have to wait for the walk?

Walking over the bridge
Terror was a clever cat
Stalking me on the wobbling bridge
Would I fall off?

Stopping for a break
Relief washed over me
Like a warm shower
I felt glad that the long journey was behind me now.

Sophie Hopkins (9)
Kingswood Parks Primary School, Kingswood

Watermelon Moon

Going in the spaceship,
Wondering what it's going to look like,
Buckling ourselves up in the humongous rocket,
Closing our eyes, praying nothing will happen,
Praying hard, hoping we won't die,
Opening our eyes,
Seeing galaxies everywhere in sight,
Arriving on the moon,
Upside down, we get out,
Climbing up the rocky moon,
We get all of our things,
Putting our things on a cloud,
Smiles on our faces when we see air boarding,
Getting in our groups, we walk over to air boarding,
Singing PGL songs all the way,
Doing a practice run,
We all get the hang of it,
Moving on to normal air boarding,
We get the hang of it.

Lillian Shakira Hamilton (11)
Kingswood Parks Primary School, Kingswood

Fun Run

The day of the fun run
Worry was an ant
Crawling in my stomach
Would I be able to carry on?

Standing on the dreaded start line
Fear was an intimidating clown
Standing in front of me
Would last place be my destiny?

Crossing the finish line
Shock hit my veins
Like a lightning bolt
Pride was a trophy on a memorable day.

Harry Wakefield (9)
Kingswood Parks Primary School, Kingswood

My Street At Christmas

Our street is quite a posh street
Say the mums in tutus,
Dads dressed up as Santa,
Children chomping on chocolate Santas.
Our street is a quiet place
Say the raining marshmallows the kids catch in their mouths,
Kids shouting, "I caught one!"
Our street is a lovely tidy place
Say the flying foxes in your garden,
Colourful tidy Christmas trees,
With huge presents underneath.
Our street is a busy street
Say the shopkeepers trying to get home,
And rude boys,
Says teacher Jim and nice Ted.
Our street is a new street
Say the clean doors and nice pavements.
But our street is the most amazing one
Says me!

Elisha-Joy Baldwin (8)
Kingswood Parks Primary School, Kingswood

My Special Street

My street is a posh place,
Say the mums in fancy dresses,
Dads in suits,
Kids in jeans.
Our street is a tidy place.

Cold weather and raining marshmallows,
Gumballs flying from one end to the other,
People squashed through their own doors.

Say the lolly wrappers, chippy bags,
And good graffiti on walls.
Our street is not a lazy place.

Rhys Harrison (8)
Kingswood Parks Primary School, Kingswood

Radical Raft

Here I am, holding the rope that's scorched,
Splash!
All I hear is a teacher with a funny giggle.

Terror shakes me as I climb onto the barrel raft,
Oars waving, making a ripple behind us.

Splash! One falls in like a starfish, circling the lake,
We get back to shore.

Dripping, a photo taken of us making memories,
Off we trudge back to base.

Alfie Samson (10)
Kingswood Parks Primary School, Kingswood

Our Street

Our street is a posh place to live,
Our street has the fresh plants, the clean bins, the well cared for grassy gardens and the polished windows,
Our street has hard pebbles,
Out street is a big one.

Our street is a new one,
Our street is a busy one,
Our street is a calm one,
Our street is a green place.

But our street is the best,
Says me.

Theodore Jones (7)
Kingswood Parks Primary School, Kingswood

Our Street

Our street is active,
Say the flying fire dragons, miraculous unicorns,
Exclusive lightning bolt rides.
Our street is awesome.

Says the sapphire-blue sea,
Zooming surfboards,
Wacky rides.
Our street is colourful.

Say the lovely ripe apples,
Growing great trees, blooming flowers.
Our street is loud.

Say our silent discos,
Dancing under the starry nights,
Noisy buffets.
Our street has lots of atmosphere.

Say the booming pool parties,
Spooky parties,

Karaoke parties till midnight.
Our street is mystical and the best.

Says me!

Ava Barley (8)
Kingswood Parks Primary School, Kingswood

The Fun Run

The day of the fun run
Excited to see where I got
Not eating anything and feeling as hungry
as a slug in my stomach
If I ate my food, would I be able to run?

Shuffling on the awful start line
Motivated like batteries were put
inside of me
Energy was flowing through me
Was I going to succeed?

In the middle of the run
I felt dizzy and I could have fallen on the floor
I needed to get a nice cool glass of
water
Could I do it?

Crossing the amazing finish line
I could feel the glory
My heart was pounding like a cheetah after a
memorable day.

Ellie-Rose Albrow (9)
Kingswood Parks Primary School, Kingswood

The Day Of The Fun Run

The day of the fun run
Nerves were taking over me
Like the poison from a snake
Would I be able to complete the race?

Standing at the start
Eagerness was running through my body
Could I come in first place?

With the finish line in my sight
I sped to the end
Exhaustion ran through me
Like diesel in a car.

Jack Drinkall (9)
Kingswood Parks Primary School, Kingswood

Fantastic Fun Run

I was at the starting line
I was shaking like a leaf
I started to leg it
All I could see was eyes stalking me.

I was determined enough to stick with it and be sick
I could see the outstanding untaken line
Would I win?

I overtook Jacob and smashed the finish line
I got the victory
My legs were jelly.

Roma Valentino Hird (9)
Kingswood Parks Primary School, Kingswood

Out Of This World PGL!

We arrived on our shuttle bus
People were frying cheese,
Making a house out of crisps
And learning to speak alien.
We got to eat lunch on the moon
First, we did hoverboarding.
Then we did hover car building
Where we had to build a
Hover car.
In the night we did
Space wars
Whoever got round the moon
In the hover car won.
Then we did boat building where
We had to sail around in the air.
We all felt very nervous for
Rock climbing. We had to
Climb up the moon and planets.
Then we had a disco where
There were lights and secrets revealed.

Amelia Rose Ainley (10)
Kingswood Parks Primary School, Kingswood

Our Street

Our street is a quiet place,
Say the wonderful houses, calm beautiful people and the hard roads.

Our street is a green place,
Say the beautiful gardens, the fresh roses and the green shiny grass.

Our street is a posh place,
Say the polished cars, clean bins and the beautiful flowers.

But our street is the best,
Says me.

Satya Hasini Giri (7)
Kingswood Parks Primary School, Kingswood

Fun Run Fear

The day of the fun run
Worry was a butterfly twisting and rolling in my stomach
Trying to get out
Would I be able to finish or carry on the race?

Standing on the black and white squared start line
Fear that I wouldn't finish and I would not get to the finish line
Was my chance good or bad?
Would I finish the race or would I be the very last person to cross the finish line?

Crossing the finish line
As the relief passed me and pride came to my mind
like a fast car which just finished an Olympic race
I passed the finish line with relief.

Sofie Marie Goralora (9)
Kingswood Parks Primary School, Kingswood

The Fun Run

I was stood at the starting line
My nerves were trying to get to me
As the run began

Shaking like a jelly
I was flying like an aeroplane
Whizzing across the field
My heart pounded like a drum

Out of nowhere
I could see the finishing line
I was running like a cheetah was behind me and I was his prey
My prey was the finishing line

I felt like the world was counting on me
For the last lap, I belted for the finishing line
I flung along the finishing line
Even though I was ill after
I was proud of myself.

Imogen Sophia Jefferson (9)
Kingswood Parks Primary School, Kingswood

The Funniest Fun Run Ever

There I was stood, waiting to race,
I took my place on the starting line,
Butterflies filled my tummy as I stepped forwards,
As I started running, my heart started to pound.

Forcefully, I made my legs run faster,
I kept stopping to catch my breath,
Dragging myself forward,
I knew I couldn't give up.

My legs felt numb,
They felt wobbly like jelly,
I felt as floppy as a pancake.

I was as proud as a peacock,
Relief filled my heart,
I didn't win, but to me I did,
Proudness flooded through my veins.

Aimee Mae Green (9)
Kingswood Parks Primary School, Kingswood

My New, Posh Street

Our street is posh,
Our street is a posh place,
The mums in dresses, dads in posh shoes,
Kids in denim jackets.

Our street is not a quiet place,
Mess-free cars getting clean with Dad's smelly feet,
Friendly neighbours partying out.

Our street is not a lazy place,
Say the racing kids and clothes getting washed by Mum,
Dad's making the pool,
Then getting a waterfall on his face,
Kids getting thrown in the pool,
And throwing water balloons everywhere,
With posh racing bikes and colourful scooters.

Olivia Brockbank (8)
Kingswood Parks Primary School, Kingswood

Our Street

Our street is a very green place,

Say the beautiful grass, clean bins and cared for gardens.
Our street is not a quiet place,

Say the barking dogs, honking bikes and children shouting.
Our street is a tidy place,

Say the lolly wrappers, beautiful walls and the pavement.
Our street is a short one,

Say milkman Jim, postman Joe and the rent man.
Our street is not a lazy place,

Say the car washing dads, clothed mums and marble boys.

But our street is the best,
Says me!

Evie Jo Ellam (7)
Kingswood Parks Primary School, Kingswood

Trip To Space

Walking along the floor,
All he could hear was the crunching of the moon rock,
Climbing up the big wall of moon,
He grabbed onto the large hole,
Making his way to the top,
The laser stood out in the dark night,
It reflected off the tall, hard moon mountains,
The fluffy clouds floated around the moon,
Showing the sparkly stars in the blank black sky.

Elissia Grace Brown (10)
Kingswood Parks Primary School, Kingswood

Our Street

On our street is a beautiful house,
And my car is next to my house,
And the little rocks are next to my house,
And the steps are next to the little rocks,
And my door and the trees are next to my house,
And the leaves are waving because the wind is blowing the leaves.

But our street is the best,
Says me!

Amelia Wisniewska (7)
Kingswood Parks Primary School, Kingswood

Our Street

Our street is totally a posh place,
Say the mums who cook magical feasts,
And dads that dance in the streets,
Our street is not a calm place,
See us cooperating together as a team,
Our street is a clean place,
See us recycling our bags,
We do not graffiti,
Our street is a calm street,
See the houses that are posh,
Playful boys and girls,
Our street has lots of tidy houses,
Says milkman Sam and postman Freddie,
Say the looked after doors and strong walls.

Says me!

Rima Saeed Alshahrani (8)
Kingswood Parks Primary School, Kingswood

Fun Run

The day of the fun run
Petrifying feelings were a clown
Racing about in the pit of my stomach with its sad face beneath the make-up
Would it be impossible to reach the end?

Standing on the monstrous start line
Fear was a fist
punching me where my hopeful heart should have been
Was I going to fail?

I leapt across the finish line
My heart had come back
The clown and the fist burst into silver confetti
Tenth place out of around forty girls wasn't so bad after all.

Gabbie Jane McDonald (10)
Kingswood Parks Primary School, Kingswood

My Posh Street

Our street is a posh place,
People in Nando's getting drunk,
Babies swimming in the stream like they just don't care,
Babies screaming when you're in bed,
They pull your hair,
Dogs that bark when you're in bed,
Shadows on the wall of dogs,
My street is the best!
Say yes!

Ellie May Woods (8)
Kingswood Parks Primary School, Kingswood

Quick Drive!

As I got my bandana on, my heart was racing,
I hopped onto the rock-hard seat, ready to go,
The engine roared like a lion.

I slowly set off, getting faster and faster,
Getting bumpier and bumpier,
Sweat dripping off my face.

Nearly falling off because I was going that fast,
Going that fast that I was drifting,
My fingers were hurting from holding the accelerator.

Bouncing all over the place,
My bandana falling down,
Nearly breathing in smoke.

Grace Dinsdale (10)
Kingswood Parks Primary School, Kingswood

Our Street

Our street is a lush green place,

Says the next door neighbour,

The green grass and leafy golden trees.

Our street has black and white cars,

Say the pupil's friends,

And the roads.

Our street does have big brown fences all over the place,

Say the strangers.

Our street is a happy place because teenagers are riding their shiny bikes,

Say the kids.

But our street is the best,

Says me!

Ethan Turner (7)
Kingswood Parks Primary School, Kingswood

The Day Of The Fun Run

The day of the fun run,
excited like a flash.
It was so quick, it lasted a millisecond
Thinking, *will I finish the race?*

Lining up on the start line,
We started.
Caught in last place,
Would I come in last place?

Halfway, I started to heavily breathe,
Jogging with no one in front of me.
Everyone cheering for me.

Crossing the finish line,
Exhausted like an engine.
Thinking I was last,
When in reality I came 52nd.

Faris Alghamdi (9)
Kingswood Parks Primary School, Kingswood

Our Street

Our street is a tidy place,

Say the mums pulling their bins out, polished cars and green grass.

Our street has a quiet road say the dads.

Our street has cream houses.

But our street is the best,

Says me!

Alex Waller (7)
Kingswood Parks Primary School, Kingswood

PGL In Space

The spaceship rattled, dodging stars
The children weren't taking notice
They were too busy munching sweets
They arrived at PGL and they
Got into their first activity
Spaceship building
They jumped joyfully
And they forgot about the gravity
They were full of pride.

Oliver Smith (10)
Kingswood Parks Primary School, Kingswood

The Fun Run

The coach raised his hand
I embraced myself
It was time to run
It was time for fun

My nerves shook
"Why stop?"
Bellowed my determination
The race started
I darted off the start line

Pain tried to drag me down but I didn't let it
I hesitated
Then darted further on
My will kept me going

I neared the end
I crossed the line
I may not have won
But I made it
Relief welled up inside of me.

Billy Drury (9)
Kingswood Parks Primary School, Kingswood

Fun Run

The day of the fun run
Worry was a butterfly - it fluttered around in my stomach
fluttering around, making me feel sick
Could I do it?

Standing on the wicked start line
nervousness filled me like a balloon
striking me. I began to tremble
Was I supposed to do it?

My stitch overwhelmed me
Other people ran by like falling raindrops
The finish line came into view
Wow, it was the sprinkles on top of the cake
I had done it!

Amelia Spicer-Matthews (9)
Kingswood Parks Primary School, Kingswood

PGL But Not PGL

Travelling to PGL,
Bananas flying high in the sky.
Arriving, the exotic feeling starting,
Bursting with excitement.
Marching on to upcoming activities.
Building the complex tech,
The easy parts and hard parts,
Resilience is key.
Finished hover car works like a charm,
Up, down, left and right.
Moving on to the next activity,
High-tech hover cars are the way.
Space wars, powerful lasers,
Make victories and memories.

Harley Marshall (10)
Kingswood Parks Primary School, Kingswood

The Mythical Unicorn

The mythical unicorn is a magical pet,

Say the fairies in mushrooms, colourful butterflies and purple birds.

The mythical unicorn is a delightful unicorn,

Say the humans in houses, ladies in living rooms and men in beds.

The mythical unicorn is not very colourful,

Say mums in kitchens, dads in beds and kids playing games.

The mythical unicorn isn't very big and magical, but it's the best!

Isabelle Marie Fellows (8)
Kingswood Parks Primary School, Kingswood

Fun Run Scare

I was on the starting line,
Waiting for the ready, steady, go,
My nerves were telling me no,
The coach shouted, "Go!"

I ran and ran,
Determination bubbled inside me,
I was chasing victory,
No one could stop me now.

Pride danced through me,
Sweat dropped off my body,
My legs were numb.

I could see the finish line,
I ran and ran,
When I finished I was so proud.

Lola Drury (9)
Kingswood Parks Primary School, Kingswood

Skater

On a magnificent cliffside stands a mega skate park

There you'll find 'The Legend'

He wears the crown of trickster king

The skating wizard performs dangerous tricks and power slides on his incredible colourful deck

On steep ramps the mega skater rides as fast as a flash

He competes using ollies, nollys and crazy backflips on the super ultra mega ramp

Are you a skater?

Benjamin Hopkins (8)
Kingswood Parks Primary School, Kingswood

Our Street

Our street is not a normal place
say aliens in dungarees
and dragons with chips.

Our street is a crazy place
say witches with potions and
the record-breaking drivers.

Our street is not a quiet place
says the Queen, F1 drivers
and the army.

Our street is a colourful place
say the hardworking dads
and robots.

But our street is just right
says me!

Dylan Harry Booker-Kingdom (8)
Kingswood Parks Primary School, Kingswood

The Fun Run

The day of the fun run.
Worry was a butterfly,
fluttering around my stomach.
Would I be able to finish this snake-like run?

Standing on the brink of the starting line.
I felt like I was going to fall off a cliff,
like I was going to fall to bits.
Was last place my only hope?

Crossing the finish line,
pride hit me,
like a bomb in my heart.
Praise was my golden ticket.

Angelina Ferriby (9)
Kingswood Parks Primary School, Kingswood

The Fun Run

The day of the fun run
Worry was a tractor
slowly ploughing the crops in my stomach
Would I be able to reach the finish line or not?

Standing on the dangerous start line
fear was consuming me
making me feel weak like a slug
Was last place where I belonged?

Crossing the finish line
Relief spread across my body
like a drag racer
finally finishing the race.

Elliott Robinson (9)
Kingswood Parks Primary School, Kingswood

My Hygenic Street

My street is a posh one
Say the boys in named clothes,
No crumbling walls,
Street isn't a lazy place,
Street is a new place,
Street has springy pavements,
Our street is the best,
Our street is a very calm place.

Charlie Stanley Waudby (8)
Kingswood Parks Primary School, Kingswood

The Clean Street

Our street is a posh place,
Say the mums in fancy dresses,
Dads in suits,
Kids in jeans,
Our street is a tidy place.

Cold weather and raining marshmallows,
Gumballs flying from one end to another,
People squashed through their own doors.

Say the lolly wrappers, chippy wrappers and,
Good drawings on walls,
Our street is not a lazy place,

Says me!

Freddie Reuben Jessop (8)
Kingswood Parks Primary School, Kingswood

My Crazy Street

At the end of my street,
A row of houses,
A house of children,
Shouting, banging,
Scratching, biting, nipping,
Sisters fighting,
Houses flooding

Houses made out of Lego,
Candyfloss houses,
Streets flooded with colour,
Kids screaming in the pools,
Mums whizzing all around,
Dads playing rugby in the car park,
Fun days in my crazy street.

Eva Brooks (8)
Kingswood Parks Primary School, Kingswood

Our Amazing Street!

Our street is not an exciting place

Says the roller coaster of life, the quiet neighbours

Our street is not an ordinary street

Says the boiling drain system
and Dad's loud coffee machine

Our house is not a quiet place

Says the crying baby and
Dad's radio

But our street is amazing

Says me!

Seth Whittaker (8)
Kingswood Parks Primary School, Kingswood

The Day Of The River Walk

The day of the river walk
Worry like a brainless goldfish
wondering what to do
Would I be able to travel that far?

Standing on the dreaded bridge
Fear was the long walk
shivering down my spine
Did I make a mistake?

On the way home
relief sped through me
like a traveller who came from afar
Tiredly, we walked back to school.

Oliver Henley (9)
Kingswood Parks Primary School, Kingswood

Our Street

Our street is a tidy one,
Says the rubbish in the bin, well cared for gardens and polished cars.
Our street is not a lazy one, with a beautiful cherry tree.
Our street has clean polished, dried windows,
But our street is the best,
Says me!

Lucas Lamplough (7)
Kingswood Parks Primary School, Kingswood

Our Street

Our street is not a posh place,
Say the mums in the big fluffy jackets,
Dads with big boots,
Kids with colourful hats.

Our street is not a quiet place,
Say the loud dogs barking,
Our honking bikes,
Our shouts.

Our street is not a tidy place,
Say the muddy paths,
The tiny, little wand shop,
The plain bricked walls.

Scarlett Azelia Taylor (8)
Kingswood Parks Primary School, Kingswood

Kingswood

Our street is not a quiet place
Say the mums in Domino's
Kids in school
Our street is a loud place
Say our football matches
Our squeaky bikes
Our calls
Our street is a lovely place
Say the lolly wrappers
Chippy bags
And written on walls
Broken trees
Our street is not a bad place

Says me.

Chloe Chapman (8)
Kingswood Parks Primary School, Kingswood

To The Moon

On the way to the moon,
The stars,
The dark sky,
The planets,
We arrived,
There was moon rock as food,
Spaceships as buildings,
Excitement filled space,
The stars,
The dark sky,
The planets,
As the instructor babbled on in an alien language.

Megan Johnson (10)
Kingswood Parks Primary School, Kingswood

Making Butterflies Out Of Tigers

You can't make a tiger,
Out of a butterfly,
But you can make a Chinese lantern.

You can't make a cobra,
Out of a butterfly,
But you can make a diamond rose.

You can't make an eagle,
Out of a butterfly,
But you can make a rainbow shine.

You can't make a parrot,
Out of a butterfly,
But you can make a copy.

You can't make a sunset,
Out of a butterfly,
But you can make a poem.

Holly Casey (10)
Maybury Primary School, Hull

Have You Ever Wondered?

Have you ever wondered why dogs bark?
How the sun decided to go to bed and allow the dark?

Have you ever wondered why knights always fight?
Or who discovered that the wind can blow a kite?

Have you ever wondered why the grass is green?
Or how Santa Claus goes around the world without being seen?

Have you ever wondered why we believe in mythical creatures,
From fire-breathing dragons to unicorns and their mystical features?

All of these wonders, to us, are one big mystery,
And I bet the answers are as useful as a barbecue under the sea.

Destynie Monkman (9)
Maybury Primary School, Hull

The Weird Dream

I had a fantastically weird dream the other night,
I dreamt that an elephant came to my ballet class to dance,
Dressed in a pink ballet tutu and shoes,
She leapt high in the air like a gazelle,
Landed like a graceful swan in the splits,
She rose up and pirouetted diagonally across the wooden floor like a fairy doll,
And balanced with her trunk high up in the air,
She left the floor with a curtsy, to thunderous cheers and applause,
The crowd threw roses and went wild with delight,
I cheered so hard I fell out of bed,
And just to prove it, I have a bump on my head.

Phoebe-Mai Jenkins (9)
Maybury Primary School, Hull

Rocket Adventure!

Skip on a rocket,
With gravity in my pocket,
Drifting around,
Miles off the ground.

Everything's floating,
I feel I should be gloating,
But no one's here in this silent atmosphere,
Space gear very near.

Excited and little fear,
Time is flying, almost here,
To feel my feet touch solid ground,
Back to Earth safe and sound.

To walk out of the amazing rocket,
To feel the gravity out of my pocket!

Ella Dockerty (11)
Maybury Primary School, Hull

Genie's Always With Me

Genie, Genie is so bright,
Genie, Genie locks me up tight,
Genie, Genie lets me go,
When it's nearly time to snow,
Snow is white, Genie's blue,
We throw snowballs at an igloo,
Genie, Genie can be a fright,
From his delight.

Olivia May Hardy (9)
Maybury Primary School, Hull

Jumping In Space

Climb aboard the spaceship, we're going to the moon,
We will be ready to set off soon.

Are you ready to jump on the moon?
To count all the stars around you?

Then we fly to Mars and when we get there,
We are exploring all of the hot volcanoes.

Then we jump to Jupiter,
We have a break and lots of fun.

Let's see Saturn with his amazing ring,
Let's have fun and do funny things.

Our last stop is Neptune, it is full of ice,
We can play hockey but my mum is talking, "Time to wake up!"

Alan Drewno (9)
Newington Academy, Hull

The Cat That Annoys Me Like That

I have a cat, his name is Willo,
He is always sleeping on my pillow,
He comes in to eat and play,
After that he runs away,
In and out, in and out,
That's what makes me want to shout,
Night-time comes, night-time goes,
The next thing I know,
He's scratching at my door,
Because he wants more,
He chases the birds,
And I do have words,
He plays with his toy mouse,
When he is in my house,
That is my cat Willo,
That sleeps on my pillow.

Savanna Thompson (9)
Newington Academy, Hull

Water Way To Travel!

I made a car out of water,
I went for a drive with my grandad's daughter,
We drove up a very big mountain,
And at the top was a very big fountain,
Then we slid down the road,
As I waved at some toads!
After I'd waved them goodbye,
We went home to dry,
I will never forget,
The day we got wet,
In my transporter,
Made of water.

Lenny Jones (9)
Newington Academy, Hull

My Weird World

There was a boy named Bob,
Who lived in a house of Hobnobs,
He lived next to an upside-down school,
That had the world record for the biggest upside-down swimming pool,
The school was next to the home of a talking cockatoo!
Next to the home of the talking cockatoo was a shop that sold poo!
Next to the shop was a place that went pop,
Next to the place that went pop there was a mop next to a sign saying, *My weird world!*

George Leason (9)
Newington Academy, Hull

What Can You Do With A Dog?

Well, you can play with it, play fetch with it,
Feed it, wash it and hug it all day,
You can buy it, you can sell it or keep it with you,
You can take it to a park, you can sleep with it,
You can take it to a dog-sitter,
You can help it, you can chase it and run all around,
You can stare at it, you can lose it, you can find it,
You can hug it one more time.
That's what you can do with a dog.

Simona Tina Vacmane (9)
Newington Academy, Hull

Cheese Moon

You see it at
night in the sky,
you might wanna take a bite.
It looks like a giant cheeseball
but it's only the cheese moon. Let's
fly a balloon to the cheese moon. Let's
eat it like a baboon. It's so great
at night seeing the sight of the
flight. Well it is only one evening
and the time of the mysterious night.
A secret no one knows is that the
cheese moon watches the bottom
of the rainbow farting
rockets that only
appear at night.

Julia Bartczak (9)
Newington Academy, Hull

A Flying Limo

I bought a limo from down the street,
It was peppermint-green,
And it belonged to the Queen,
I drove it around the corner,
I went too fast and the wheels went *bang!*
And the wings came out,
It flew to the sky,
I didn't know it was a magical car,
I flew it in the sky,
As the birds went by,
I flew through the clouds to a magical land,
In the Land of Make Believe,
Where I met the Sandman,
And realised it was all a dream.

Amber Scaum (9)
Newington Academy, Hull

Lazy Mushroom

I'm a little mushroom and I love sleeping and I'm very lazy.
I hate being woken up, so I sleep underground.
Nobody likes me because I'm grumpy and mean.
No one comes near me because I angrily stomp.
I wake up for eating and that's about it.
Oh I forgot about the shops.
I've got to get food for the rest of the month.

Wiktor Skorupa (9)
Newington Academy, Hull

Creature Of The Night

There it lies on a dark, dark night,
Covered in black, not a bit of white,
See its eyes glowing and shining,
Hear it yelping and whining,
I hear it whining every night,
Get out of bed and turn on my light,
Look out of my window and what do I see?
Nothing but moonlight shining on me.

Ben Leeman (9)
Newington Academy, Hull

Underwater Football

Underwater football, crazy show,
I play with my friends to the moon and back,
The waves don't beat us, the sharks don't scare us,
We will be champions and we will play to the end,
We jump and swim, we take our adventure every day,
Passion and power, we sometimes feel like a long shower.

Nataniel Zoch (10)
Newington Academy, Hull

Cars

I went for a drive in my car,
I didn't get very far,
I ran out of fuel,
And I thought I was cool,
I had my sunglasses on,
And I did a very big yawn,
And then I went to bed,
And that's all I said.

Mackennya Wilkinson (9)
Newington Academy, Hull

Volcanos

V olcanos are erupting
O n the mountains, lava is dripping
L and trees are being burnt down
C haos fireworks coming out
A shy clouds in the blue sky
N asty red rocks flying out into the toxic sky
O utstanding noises and banging
S ilence as the volcano calms down.

Mason Jameson (10)
Newington Academy, Hull

Apple Crumble

When my belly rumbles,
I eat an apple crumble,
I munch a whole piece,
And find my tickets to Greece,
I pack my suitcases and off I go,
High on the plane I go, go, go,
I land in Greece, then go to the beach,
I meet my friend and we eat an apple crumble each!

Oliwia Styga (10)
Newington Academy, Hull

Lions

Leaping and sleeping,
Oval manes and straight whiskers,
I saw lions sleeping beside me,
Noble animals indeed!
Sleeping lions.

Matthew James Bateman (9)
Newington Academy, Hull

Unicorn

There once was a unicorn,
It had a very shiny horn,
Every day for a treat,
It liked to eat something sweet,
It lived in an enchanted forest,
Every day at dawn,
The sunrise woke up this unicorn.

Alexa Simpson (9)
Newington Academy, Hull

Tea With A Dinosaur

I had a dinosaur round for tea,
He decided to turn up at quarter past three,
It was not like him to be so late,
But I let him off,
He is my best mate!

Charlie James Kennedy (9)
Newington Academy, Hull

Curious Carrot In A Rickety Rocket

One fascinating day, I was driving down the lane,
My mum shouted, "Carrot in a rocket!" I thought she was insane,
But then I swiftly saw something disintegrate in the sky,
Then I found out through the bubblegum clouds that she wasn't telling a lie,
A bubbling bonanza carrot was flying in the sky!
I punched myself to see if I was dreaming,
Sun still facing me gleaming,
Then I knew it was really real,
Flying the rocket made out of steel,
When I arrived back at home, the flabagastic carrot crashed,
Flying through the sky the ripped up rocket was beaten and mashed,
Suddenly the carrot landed in my back garden,
"What the heck?" I screeched with a reply,
"I beg your pardon!"

Farren Roper (10)
St Andrew's CE Primary School, Sutton Park

The Unicorn And The Mushroom

Something awaited me, something very strange,
There really was quite a range,
A rainbowtastic unicorn was eating a sausagtastic rainbow sausage,
It really made a trumpbollistic rainbow,
The air started to fill with an oxygenated smell,
Which put the garden in to a candylicious spell,
From a fabulous smell to a taste of candy that rang a bell.

Suddenly, something strange happened again,
Something brain tingling baffled me like one to ten,
A mushroom, a galaxy mushroom, was riding a teaspoon,
Over the astronicious moon,
Finding its way over a rainbow of clouds,
Disappeared into mounds.

Strange things happened,
But this really didn't happen,

I drifted off to sleep again,
Before it was time to wake up from this dream again,
I wished it would just come true!

Ellie Walker (11)
St Andrew's CE Primary School, Sutton Park

The Unicorn And The Pig

Tanka Poetry

Once there was a pig
A pig, one pig, all alone,
Once there was a pig,
On the muddylicious farm,
On the muddylicious farm.

Flying from above,
There was a big unicorn,
Flying from above,
A trail of rainbow sparkles,
A trail of rainbow sparkles.

"Come for lunch," he said,
Fish and chips for lunch, yum, yum,
"Come for lunch," he said,
"On my rainbow of Skittles,
On my rainbow of Skittles."

Pig had a good time,
Tea and biscuits for supper,
Pig had a very good time!

Jasmine Molloy (10)
St Andrew's CE Primary School, Sutton Park

Candy Problems

Gummy bear, gummy bear
Please go away
Gummy bear, gummy bear
I don't want you to stay

You've chased me all day long
Gummy bear, gummy bear
I've done nothing wrong!
Gummy bear, gummy bear
There's something in the blue
Gummy bear, gummy bear
It's not one of you

It's a cola bottle
That's running to me at full throttle

Cola bottle, cola bottle
Please go away
Cola bottle, cola bottle
I don't want you to stay
Argh!

Elicia JLJ Spivey (10)
St Andrew's CE Primary School, Sutton Park

The Aerial World

I don't get this world,
Everything is getting hurled.
Cars and boats and balloons,
Trains, helicopters and buses too.

As you can really see,
This is the place to be.
It's in space, don't you know?
Where vehicles move and go.

In Vehicle City,
Some friends are staying with me.
And also what's more,
Different kinds of people galore.

I'm sorry I have to go back,
I guess I'll have to go pack.
I think that we...
Could be friends forever, don't you see?

Andrew Opene (10)
St Andrew's CE Primary School, Sutton Park

Bushy Ball

The unstoppable keeper was a bushy one,
How hairy could he be?
There was only one way,
To win the game,
To make him go on his knees,
His hair was matted brown,
We were determined to knock him down,
I found a candy cane in his mane,
He would never play football again.

The next game, we had got even better,
His hair was even wetter,
We whacked a hose,
On his nose,
The wet mane was never the same,
He got the blame,
That they had lost the game
He never tried again!

Harry Moon (10)
St Andrew's CE Primary School, Sutton Park

Lava Fun

I clambered to the top of the volcano,
About to have some fun.
When something started to rumble,
I knew that I was in trouble.
At that moment, I needed to run,
But guess what?
The lava started to flow.
I didn't know what to do,
So I stood up to see what would happen,
Before I knew it, I was pretty much at the bottom.
I climbed the volcano just to have some fun,
And I'll tell you something, I had such a time.
By the time I had reached the bottom,
I was as hyped as never before.
Then I started to climb back up again just for more.

Olivia Christine Fullard (10)
St Andrew's CE Primary School, Sutton Park

Never Judge A Book By Its Cover!

I stepped through a door and what did I see?
I saw something that would change me.
I turned around and looked at the sign,
It was Wonderland Poetry,
It looked so divine.
I looked over the hill, oh no what was that?
And then I saw it was a half-eaten candy bat.
It sat on a toadstool,
Then jumped into a fruitilicious pool,
Oh what was I thinking?
Why was I scared?
It turned into a beautiful pink bird,
This place was amazing,
I didn't want to leave,
Oh Wonderland Poetry why do you have to be so extreme?

Emily Myers (10)
St Andrew's CE Primary School, Sutton Park

Millions Of Sausages

Millions of sausages
Falling from the air
Millions of sausages
Fall onto my chair

They fall into my mouth
From way up in the sky
They fall into my mouth
I put on my sausage tie

Sausages are tasty
I eat them all the time
Sausages are tasty
They're better than a lime

Millions of sausages
Falling from the air
Millions of sausages
Fall onto my chair.

Samuel Paul Jordan (10)
St Andrew's CE Primary School, Sutton Park

Candy Zoo

I climbed up some stairs so high,
To hear the sound of an animal's cry,
When I reached the top,
There was a loud bubblegum pop!
And tall candy cane gates,
Leading me to my animal mates,
As soon as I walked in,
There was a large fish fin,
Followed by a shark,
With a big bite mark,
But then I came to an end,
To fall off a bend,
I landed on a cloud,
To be loud,
To find a giant bed,
To rest my sleepy head.

Harlie (10) & Grace McKenzie
St Andrew's CE Primary School, Sutton Park

Harry The Haribo

A Haribo went to a human school one day

H arry was his name
A nd he was the smartest in the school
R unning happily to his classes
I n class he just showed how happy he was
B ut one day, he started to get bullied
O bviously he told straight away

G oing on in time, he stopped getting bullied
O n his table in class he had lots of fun
E veryone asked him for help
S o he just helped them

T oys after work made him have more detailed answers
O nwards in time, he had harder questions

S o he worked harder than ever
C oolness did not help him
H arry loved school
O h so much
O nomatopoeia was his thing in literacy
L oved that his school was in the air.

Harry Busby (10)
St Andrew's CE Primary School, Sutton Park

Underwater Go Down Low!

U nderwater is the place to be
N ot when you're above the sea
D own below, a game takes place
E veryone is in the race
R un around the building to help you win
W hatever you do, never go near the bin
A ctive as ever it may be
T ake your time below the sea
E very step along the way
R ight or left every day

V ideo games are in the sea
I n the sea, anything can be
D own below is a magical place
E very day there's a secret base
O ver the bridge, under the water you may chase!

G enies can help you along the way
A pparently they race every day
M agical as ever it can get
E verybody makes a bet...

Ruby Grace Agnew (10)
St Andrew's CE Primary School, Sutton Park

Hot Tub Of Wonder

Delicious scent of hot chocolate filled the air,
Mouthwatering chocolate filled my nose while I was swinging in my chair,
Dipping my feet in the chocolicious tub,
I jumped right in and began to scrub,
Scrumptious chocolate, gulping it down,
After that hot tub, I don't think I'll ever frown,
The chocolate was so creamy,
The heat of it so steamy,
And the taste was nice and dreamy,
In the hot tub relaxing,
Lying in the sun chillaxing.

Dylan Smith (10)
St Andrew's CE Primary School, Sutton Park

Unicorn Dream

Yesterday was a very magical day,
It was different in one mysterious way,
I fell deep into a dark hole,
Following a big fat mole.

I couldn't believe what I saw,
Surely the creature was breaking a law.

A unicorn was pooping glitter into the sky,
I really couldn't understand why.

Before I could even shut my eyes,
I was surfing on rainbows in the sky.

Graicee-Ella Caulfield (10)
St Andrew's CE Primary School, Sutton Park

Mysterious Carrot

There was a flash of lightning,
"Oh what was that?"
I was sat on a train with a carrot at the wheel,
It turned around and said, "Hello!"
And then popped into a marshmallow,
The train set off,
But who was driving?
It was the carrot from the start all over again,
Another flash of lightning hit me again,
But I woke up in my bed,
With a carrot in my head,
What was happening?

Adam Taylor (10)
St Andrew's CE Primary School, Sutton Park

Walking Doggy

I was taking my dog for a walk,
Suddenly, I fell in a lava hole,
Then my dog went missing,
I put a sign up for help,
All I need is my dog and me,
I've been crying all day,
Trying to figure out a way,
There is one thing that will make my day,
That is my dog being here today,
I wish my dog was here now,
So we can play again,
If only I had my great dog, Ben.

Callum Barley (10)
St Andrew's CE Primary School, Sutton Park

Mermazing

M um took Evie and Codie to the beach. Swimming in the blue sea, Evie got dragged into the water by a beautiful mermaid called Ruby.
E vie was amazed. She looked at her legs and she had a mermaid tail!
R uby came up to the top of the water and saw a girl named Codie.
M um wondered where Evie and Codie were so she went to look for them but she couldn't find them.
A nd Evie was having so much fun exploring and swimming. So was Codie!
"I wonder where Evie and Codie are. I hope they are okay," babbled Mum, looking puzzled.
D ad phoned Mum to say that the girls were safe and having a mermazing time.

Codie Hewick (11)
St Andrew's CE Primary School, Sutton Park

Candy Cane Gang

I found a candy cane,
It hit me in the vein
I got a hook,
And hit it in the nook,
He was as alive as you and me,
It attacked everyone it could see,
I followed it into a tepee,
There I saw three,
More candy canes ready to attack,
I used my mighty sword. *Crack!*
That was the end of the horrible gang,
Bang, bang, bang!

Harry Rudkin (10)
St Andrew's CE Primary School, Sutton Park

The Magical Tree

There once was a magical tree
Which was only meant for me,
I began to climb
I saw a dime,
It blew in the breeze
And landed on my knees,
I climbed back down
With a frown,
Then I went in the house
I met a mouse,
The mouse ate the dime
Which was truly a crime,
I won't lie
I started to cry.

Millie Jane Stewart (10)
St Andrew's CE Primary School, Sutton Park

The Changing World

After many days,
I was in a haze,
Then I found myself in a maze,
Soon I fell into a daze.

I ate chocolate which I hate,
Then I found myself with my mate,
Whilst I was on a date,
It was great!

The next day I was looking at a light,
It gave me a fright,
I thought I might,
Test my sight.

Alex Tarsey (10)
St Andrew's CE Primary School, Sutton Park

Fortnite

I played on Fortnite
and I was on it all night.
I got told off
I got caught.
Then I was taught
not to go on my game
and search for fame.
I waited on the shelf
and met an elf.
He took me to Santa
and asked for banter.
We had a few laughs
and saw giraffes.

Ava Grace Pearson (10)
St Andrew's CE Primary School, Sutton Park

Applesnal Vs Applepool

A pplefield is full of our best players
P ineapple runs down the wing, shoots and scores
P ineapple makes it one nil to Applesnal
L etting the ball go past Applelet, Apple Van Dijk clears it
E ventually it is half-time and our Apple players go away
S uddenly, Applefield is all hyped, ready for the next half to begin
N early time for the half, but it has to start again
A pplefield are having a boring time until Pineapple scores again
L eaving the fantastic stadium, Applesnal are victorious and Applepool are shocked.

Connor David Vass (10)
St Andrew's CE Primary School, Sutton Park

My Scary Roam

A large green crocodile nibbled on my shoe,
Even worse, they were new,
I had no idea what it was doing,
I hoped it wasn't pooing!
Then it ate a doughnut with its big jaws,
It growled, "I want more!"
"Oh no, I'm a mouse,
I need my Pegasus, Clouse."
He gave me a ride home,
What a great roam.

Lauren Longley (10)
St Andrew's CE Primary School, Sutton Park

The Perfect Summer

The sky was so bright,
The sun so light,
I jumped in the pool,
To make myself cool,
Then I turned red,
I went to my bed,
My body was in pain,
Then it started to rain,
One day I went to the park,
Then my friends and I had a lark,
Soon it became dark,
The stars started to spark.

Lily Elizabeth Emma Russell (10)
St Andrew's CE Primary School, Sutton Park

Richest Goldfish In The World

G ood to be rich
O ut of this world, you can get anything you want
L ovely cars
D readfully good speed
F lying down the highway
I ncredibly big houses
S pecial memories
H ouses with swimming pools

I nteresting, kind of
S uper holidays

R oarsome adventures
I ncredible amount of bank cards
C hill minds
H ouses beyond your wildest dreams

But one day his time came,
He went outside without water.

Oscar Jools Foley (10)
St Andrew's CE Primary School, Sutton Park

Roast Potato!

Once upon a time, a long time ago
There was an old, warty hairdresser potato
Unicorn walked to the salon one day
She asked Potato to cut her hair, he answered, "I may."
Snip, snap, here and there
Unicorn was left with no hair
That very night at the underwater barbecue
He was served a roast potato from me and you!

Poppy Blanchard (10)
St Andrew's CE Primary School, Sutton Park

Potato

I had a potato and took it to the vet,
They said it was horrible and wet,
The cure was to visit the Asda shop,
To find a magical ice pop,
I couldn't find it,
So I decided to sit,
I waited on a shelf,
And met an elf,
My potato was cured that day!
I was so happy in every way.

Kaiden Riley (10)
St Andrew's CE Primary School, Sutton Park

Crocimouse

A crocodile in a pink fairy dress,
Looked a very ugly mess,
She went to the coffee shop,
In her pretty pink flip-flops,
She bit into her doughnut,
She realised the flavour was coconut.

She turned into a mouse in a suit,
And she didn't like her boat,
She squeaked, "Why am I a mouse?
I can't find my house!"
She called for her Pegasus,
"That doughnut was delicious,
I want to go home!" she shouted.

Alexis Bottomley (10)
St Andrew's CE Primary School, Sutton Park

The Roasting Revenge

Philomena, the gorgeous unicorn, journeyed to get her hair cut one day,
She asked the warty potato hairdresser and he said, "I may."
The evil potato cut off all her hair
Suddenly, she started acting like a bear,
That very night, there was an underwater barbecue,
But all the unicorn did was chase the potato shouting, "Get back here you!"
Finally, Potato was put on the grill,
Philomena celebrated her revenge on the hill.

Evie Grace Hussey (10)
St Andrew's CE Primary School, Sutton Park

Strange Times

Last night, I was tucked up in bed,
To rest my sleepy head,
But then I woke up,
To find myself holding a teacup,
Then the next day, I had a feather in my mouth,
Which was facing south,
It wasn't just a feather,
It was made out of leather,
It made me clever.

William Talbot (10) & Jay Logan Johnson
St Andrew's CE Primary School, Sutton Park

Crazy Crocodile

C rocodile Oscar was in a coffee shop
R eally he was there for a brownie
O scar took a bite and turned into a...
C olourful mouse in a pink shiny tutu
O scar went outside and there was a...
D olphin rainbow Pegasus unicorn in a river
I t shouted, "Get on my back, I'll take you..."
L ouis the dolphin took him home
E ating that brownie was a regret.

Harris Chapman (10)
St Andrew's CE Primary School, Sutton Park

Love My Kitty

I love my kitten,
She is so little and cute.
She has a white tongue,
And a lot of little whiskers too.
She purrs when you stroke her back,
She usually hides in my red cap.
I always say, "Cat in the hat."
We expose her to joy.

Myles Alan Micheal McCloud (10)
St Andrew's CE Primary School, Sutton Park

Making A Dragon Out Of Potatoes

Dragons riding in the night sky,
So fierce, I wonder why,
Eating meat so very dry,
I want you to know,
I would make one out of snow,
One day I awoke,
For I was in awe,
I heard my mum snore,
I screamed galore,
There was a dragon,
As big as a kraken,
It was very mushy,
It looked like a slushy,
It was made of potatoes,
With a weird kind of nose,
I wondered how it grew.

Alfie Brennan (10)
St Andrew's CE Primary School, Sutton Park

My Donkey

My donkey is super,
He surely will blow your mind,
Sometimes he can be a nightmare,
Don't worry, he is kind.

We sit him on a stool,
And he is very cool,
The donkey plays the piano,
And he is an expert, hooray!

Joshua Horne (10)
St Andrew's CE Primary School, Sutton Park

Colourful Sheep

R ainbow, colourful sheep
A te a unicorn
I n his sleep
"N o! Don't eat a miaowing cow!"
B oom!
O n switched a light bulb
W hich showed a man having a...

S hower!
H e screamed as he got...
E aten for a sheepy supper!
E ach person in the house sprinted out
P arp! The sheep farted!

Megan Hall (10)
St Andrew's CE Primary School, Sutton Park

Weird, Wacky Wonderland

- **H** ome, playing football
- **O** n some fresh icing
- **R** euben, Archie and Breana fall down a hole by the goal
- **S** uddenly they are horsemen and a uniwoman
- **E** ntering a grassland world with a pond
- **M** ermaids pull them down into the wet murky depths
- **A** nd then they are turned into mermaids and mermen
- **N** ow they are hosting a massive underwater barbecue!

Reuben Hawkes (10)
St Andrew's CE Primary School, Sutton Park

Today Is Crazy

T oday has been weird
O n the biscuit tin was a mole
D oris was her name
A mazingly I shrunk
Y ou know she let me in

I t was massive inside the biscuit tin
S o I went in

C razy it was
R eally I was confuddled
A mazingly it was a dream
Z zzz
Y ou know what, maybe it was not.

Mia Violet Lydon (11) & Mia-Ren
St Andrew's CE Primary School, Sutton Park

Crazy Sheep

Why oh why am I a rainbow sheep?
I ate a unicorn in my sleep,
Oh why oh why am I a crazy sheep?
I ate a cow that went, "Miaow!"
Oh why am I a fluffy sheep?
I ate a mime who had no time,
Oh why am I a normal sheep?

Lily Bunby (10)
St Andrew's CE Primary School, Sutton Park

Football In Candy Land

F ootball players run on sweet cotton candy grass
O val balls fly into the strawberry lace net
O xygen surrounds the players
T all players boot the gummy ball
B alls of gummy get eaten within seconds
A ll of the players dive on the sweet grass
L ovely liquorice lines on the field
L ovely lights beam upon star players.

Archie Quest (10)
St Andrew's CE Primary School, Sutton Park

Clouds Of Candyfloss

I clambered up the clouds,
Just to have some fun,
But all of a sudden,
I heard the clouds pop like popping candy,
I knew something was wrong,
Glass birds flew past me,
And started creating a rainbow around me,
What could be more fun?
Approaching me were more clouds as candyfloss,
I jumped onto them,
And I started sinking through.

Evie-Louise Jay (10)
St Andrew's CE Primary School, Sutton Park

Tanner Fox

T anner Fox
A hamburger
N ow jumps off a pier
N ow he eats all of the candyfloss
E very day he goes to the mysterious beach
R ound and round he goes in the bowl

F ox is his last name
O ver the box he jumps
X -up is his best trick.

Jaidyn Foster (10)
St Andrew's CE Primary School, Sutton Park

Magic Mermaids

M agical, marvellous mermaids rule the sea
E ach and every day
R ight now, they're having a barbecue
M adness I would say
A lthough I know they're a myth
I 'm very special myself
D on't judge me
S till, I'm a magic unicorn.

Breanna Leigh Johnson (10)
St Andrew's CE Primary School, Sutton Park

Mushrooms Are The Best

M ushrooms are the best
U p and down they swim
S hooting through the calm water
H urtling into things
R oom for a unicorn
O n his back
O n no, the unicorn falls
M y gosh, what was that?
S ome wings pop up, it is the unicorn.

Holly Richardson (10)
St Andrew's CE Primary School, Sutton Park

Marshmallow City

Haiku Poetry

Marshmallow City!
It was fandabbydozy!
I *love* marshmallows!

It was so tasty!
My dream had come true today.
Marshmallow City!

Alex McNamara (10)
St Andrew's CE Primary School, Sutton Park

The Potato Who Climbed Too High

P otatoes climbed on the Empire State Building
"O h no, Mr FBI Chair come!"
T he FBI Chair said, "Come down"
A nd a tomato came too
T ogether they thought of a plan
"O h, the potato's run out of charge, let's run!"

Jay Keal (10)
St Andrew's CE Primary School, Sutton Park

Lazy Crocodile

Crocodile in a fairy dress
Rich but it's too stressed
Oh it's very small
Crocodiles are very tall
It is eating a doughnut from a pot and this
Doughnut is very hot
It is now a mouse and has
Lost his big mouth
Eating no hot doughnuts ever again.

Jack Dunn (11)
St Andrew's CE Primary School, Sutton Park

The Fish Playing Football

Underwater was,
A fish playing football with,
A shark chasing snails,
Playing unfairly again,
Towards the little fish.

Underwater was,
A worm playing basketball,
With a mean turtle,
Playing mean as usual,
Towards the little fish.

Rio Kassim (10)
St Andrew's CE Primary School, Sutton Park

The Strange Day

The other day was strange,
I shrank down to the size of an ant,
I was smaller than a plant,
I went into my house,
And saw a mouse,
It tried to attack me,
It hurt my knee,
And my name is Lee.

Finlay Jaydon Mortimer (10)
St Andrew's CE Primary School, Sutton Park

Santa On A Jet Ski

S anta, Santa why once a year?
A nd you are so special
N aughty Santa you are so mean
T renches is where Santa likes to go
A nd happy New Year!

William Wilson (10)
St Andrew's CE Primary School, Sutton Park

Racing A Cheetah

One day, a cheetah asked for a race
He said, "I've got a lot of pace."
"I want to see this, but you're probably lying,
But I'll take any chance I can take."
Then he proved me wrong like a piece of cake,
Then he beat me,
"Can you teach me to be better than you?"
"We're in the cat family,
You have to be manly,
But you're never gonna win like that,
You run like a two-legged rat."
I said, "I want a rematch."
But he said, "You're never going to beat that."
So I walked away,
Then I met him another day,
Then I raced the cheetah.

Harris Adamson (10)
Stoneferry Primary School, Hull

Getting My Hair Cut By A Tiger

Yesterday, I went to the jungle,
I found a seat to sit on,
Then I jumped off it and landed on the ground,
I thought it was fun!
Then along came a tiger cub,
I was excited to meet a tiger cub,
It roared to me that its name was Lila,
She told me to be her bud,
I said yes and took off my hood,
"Let's play hairdressers. I will be the hairdresser, I know how to hair dress."
I said, "Yes!"
"Let's go!" shouted Lila.
I didn't want to hurt her feelings so I said yes instead of no,
Lila said, "Sit down, now!"
"But I can't because there is a wall and I can't jump over it, it's not low."
She sliced off my hair too short,

She got my skin, "Ow!"
I shouldn't have done it, I regret it now!

Jessica Meara (10)
Stoneferry Primary School, Hull

Pigging Around!

Yes! I was in space,
My pig partner was jamming to a base,
I was just popping balloons, pigging around,
Oh no! My pig partner was going out of bounds,
I went as fast as I could,
But to my surprise, I heard a giant thud,
A meteor hit my bud,
And pushed him back into the ship,
"Ow!" Something hit my hip,
Looked like the meteor had hit me too,
"No! What am I going to do?"
The next day, I woke up in a hospital,
The doctor was talking to someone, "Yeah, that'll be a pound."
He came over to me and said, "You're fine, you were only pigging around."

Jake Peter Goforth (10)
Stoneferry Primary School, Hull

The Flying Cake

Last night I did a quick bake,
So I ended up with a giant cake,
It flew and flew until curfew,
Where it played and played,
And moved and swayed,
I jumped on it for a ride,
Then it moved from side to side,
Then it took me up to space,
To have a race,
In all its grace,
It went super fast,
And we were home at last,
At home,
Without a groan,
Me and the cake,
Began to bake.

James Bailey (10)
Stoneferry Primary School, Hull

Riding On Clouds

Riding on clouds that felt like cotton candy,
but it was just annoying my sister, Mandy.
Riding fast felt really good,
but not when it was raining mud.
It started raining lots of money,
but it wasn't that funny.
A solid gold bar landed on my head,
my friend thought I was dead.
I wished I stayed on longer,
but I really had to wander.
Then I had to go,
because it was going to snow.
Then I saw a dog,
that was on a bog.

Bradley Corran (10)
Stoneferry Primary School, Hull

Inside A Video Game

Inside a game called Super Mario,
I couldn't get out,
What could I do?
Break it?
Smash it?
I could see Mario,
He was red, rich and famous,
He flew down to me,
He said, "Do you need help?"
He said, "Do you want a ride?"
He said, "Do you want to get out?"
When we went out, a dragon came,
He smelt like smelly dribble and was wet,
I punched him in the blue belly,
My hand turned red and he had a life,
My mum came, mad, mischievous,
She was turning off the TV,
Shutting down the game in,
Three, two, one, zero,
I was safe but sad I couldn't go back,
I woke up, it was just a dream.

Leonardo de Castro Ferreira (10)
Stoneferry Primary School, Hull

Jump On A Satellite

Once there was a satellite
and there was a man that
jumped on it
the satellite shook
and had a big bump

The satellite rocked
from side to side
it caused the man to fly
into the sky

The man flew into
the stars shimmering
glistening moon and whacked his head
it bled and felt like wet bread.

Brett Craig (10)
Stoneferry Primary School, Hull

Sunbathing On Jelly

One early afternoon, I tried to fix my roof,
And I fell and landed on jelly,
I am not lying, it's the truth.

I started to wiggle and wobble as I sunk,
Cold jelly on my back,
I wanted to give it a whack.

Jiggly, tasty jelly, I needed to go,
Because it was about to snow.

Jelly was tasty, smooth and delicious,
Wibbly, wiggly.

Alfie Wadsworth (10)
Stoneferry Primary School, Hull

Playing In Dangerous Territory

I once went for a stroll
I was picking my mole
I went through a door
I heard a Phoenix go, "Caw, caw!"
The next minute, I was playing an odd game
I thought it was lame
Until the flying sharks came
Then it was the Quidditch game
My team was winning by ten points
"Ow, my joints!"
Then I caught the Snitch
The sharks fell in a ditch.

Victoria Payne (10)
Stoneferry Primary School, Hull

The Boxing Kangaroo

One day, I stumbled across a kangaroo,
He wanted to fight but I didn't want to,
The kangaroo hit me in the back of the head,
And I thought for a moment I was dead,
Then he hit me in the chin and the back,
He almost hit me everywhere and it gave a crack,
I said to him, "Stop hitting me!"
But he didn't want to,
He started using gloves,
But I was still out of puff.

Joshua Lee Stonehouse (10)
Stoneferry Primary School, Hull

Living In A Lego Block

One day, I was playing with my Lego.
All of a sudden, I started to shrink.
I was wondering what was happening.
After that, I couldn't see a thing.
My dad called me for my tea.
I shouted at the top of my tiny lungs but he didn't hear a peep out of me.
Living in a Lego block.

Tyler Wadsworth (10)
Stoneferry Primary School, Hull

Swimming With A Mermaid

Today I swam with my friend, she is scaly and really nice.
She loves human things and her favourite food is wings.
Her name is Kelly, she also loves jelly.
Kelly loves yellow and to bellow.
She's cute like a puppy and also my buddy.
Kelly has a pet called Shelly and she dropped her welly.
Her sister is called Berry and she loves her telly.
My best friend is a mermaid and she's the best friend I've ever made.

Megan Rose Taylor (10)
Stoneferry Primary School, Hull

Falling In A Toilet With A Pig

I was bursting to go to the toilet,
I was running and dancing a jig,
I had to get to the toilet,
But I bumped into a pig,
I said, "Off we go!"
Then we started to fall,
Into the enormous loo,
"Help me!" I started to call...

Riley Robert Pearce (10)
Stoneferry Primary School, Hull

Fly With A Dragon

I see clouds,
I hear wind,
As I fly through the sky on the back of a big dragon,
I feel the dragon when it's breathing,
And the skin is hot and warm,
The tail is long and thin,
Fire in the sky from the dragon's mouth.

Ema Sava (10)
Stoneferry Primary School, Hull

Young Writers Information

We hope you have enjoyed reading this book – and that you will continue to in the coming years.

If you're a young writer who enjoys reading and creative writing, or the parent of an enthusiastic poet or story writer, do visit our website www.youngwriters.co.uk. Here you will find free competitions, workshops and games, as well as recommended reads, a poetry glossary and our blog. There's lots to keep budding writers motivated to write!

If you would like to order further copies of this book, or any of our other titles, then please give us a call or visit www.youngwriters.co.uk.

Young Writers
Remus House
Coltsfoot Drive
Peterborough
PE2 9BF
(01733) 890066
info@youngwriters.co.uk

Join in the conversation!
Tips, news, giveaways and much more!

YoungWritersUK   @YoungWritersCW